Funmi Noah lives in London, United Kingdom, with her three children. Her day job is in health care. In her spare time, she likes writing, reading, walking, spa and meeting with friends. She has a special interest in patients'/carers' experiences and in charity/fundraising. *Memoir of Resilience and Hope* is her first published work.

Dedicated to you…for that hope in you, to forge ahead…to rise above all rubbles!

Funmi Noah

Rising from the Rubbles – Memoir of Resilience and Hope

Austin Macauley Publishers

LONDON • CAMBRIDGE • NEW YORK • SHARJAH

Copyright © Funmi Noah 2022

The right of Funmi Noah to be identified as author of this work has been asserted by the author in accordance with sections 77 and 78 of the Copyright, Designs and Patents Act 1988.

All rights reserved. No part of this publication may be reproduced, stored in a retrieval system, or transmitted in any form or by any means, electronic, mechanical, photocopying, recording, or otherwise, without the prior permission of the publishers.

Any person who commits any unauthorised act in relation to this publication may be liable to criminal prosecution and civil claims for damages.

All of the events in this memoir are true to the best of author's memory. The views expressed in this memoir are solely those of the author.

A CIP catalogue record for this title is available from the British Library.

ISBN 9781398453012 (Paperback)
ISBN 9781398453029 (ePub e-book)

www.austinmacauley.com

First Published 2022
Austin Macauley Publishers Ltd®
1 Canada Square
Canary Wharf
London
E14 5AA

I acknowledge God Almighty for being my all in all.

I acknowledge my family, friends and colleagues whose shoulders I have leaned on over these years.

I acknowledge my neighbours and my community for the simple smiles and nods that have cheered me on.

I acknowledge the publisher who has found the potential in this piece of work.

And I acknowledge you… the reader… for your interest in reading this book.

Table of Contents

Prologue	13
Chapter 1: The Crash – A Bang Long Coming!	16
Chapter 2: Sorting Through the Rubbles – Finding the Pieces!	25
Chapter 3: Getting Up and Looking Up – The Sun Still Shines! (Carrying My Baggage with Acceptance!)	30
Chapter 4: Restructuring and Regrouping	36
Chapter 5: Watering and Raising My Seeds – Fostering the Children	45
Chapter 6: The Voices of Hope	51
Chapter 7: Looking Back – I Am Grateful	55
Chapter 8: One Day at a Time! – The Journey Continues!	60

"Life isn't about waiting for the storm to pass. It's about learning to dance in the rain." – Vivian Greene

"My barn having burned down, I can now see the moon." – Mizuta Masahide (17th century Japanese poet and samurai)

"Rock bottom became the solid foundation in which I rebuilt my life." – J.K Rowling

"The oak fought the wind and was broken, the willow bent when it must and survived." – Robert Jordan (The Fires of Heaven)

"Life doesn't get easier or more forgiving, we get stronger and more resilient." – Steve Maraboli

"Like tiny seeds with potent power to push through tough ground and become mighty trees, we hold innate reserves of unimaginable strength. We are resilient." – Catherine DeVrye (The Gift of Nature)

"That which does not kill us, makes us stronger." – Friedrich Nietzsche

"But those who hope in the Lord will renew their strength. They will soar on wings like eagles; they will run and not grow weary, they will walk and not be faint." – Isaiah 40:31

"Hope is important because it can make the present moment less difficult to bear. If we believe that tomorrow will be better, we can bear a hardship today." – Thich Nhat Hahn

"May the God of hope fill you with all joy and peace as you trust him, so that you may overflow with hope by the power of the Holy Spirit." – Romans 15:13

Author's Note

This memoir has a lot to do with picking the pieces and rising from the crisis, than it's to do with the actual crash itself! The unflinching determination of humans to survive in the face of adversities... when everything you believed in had crumbled... when you do not know where to turn or who to trust... the strength to get up from that bed and keep on going when you've lost your drive and zest and you'd rather remain asleep... the motivation to take the next step when your vision and reality are blurred and you do not know or cannot see where you are going.

This work is dedicated to the millions of men and women, old and young, all over the world, experiencing one crisis or another. Holding on to dear life is all we can do... maybe... just maybe; the light will shine or shine better round the corner! It's the grace to survive life's crisis that would have otherwise broken you down physically and particularly mentally! The grace to retain or regain your sanity under difficult circumstances! The resilience! The hope! To find your way back to life through the rubbles!

Prologue

It's a Friday evening... the last day of September... we had only just transitioned from summer few weeks earlier... the Autumn season had started to settle in... the temperature was growing colder...the tree leaves were starting to change colours a little and our own lives were about to change forever!

I had cleaned the house that day on return from work, emptied the bin, put groceries and food shopping in the appropriate places. I had decided not to leave the house with much stuff; I wanted to see if I could start afresh and begin to create new memories. I decided that our clothing would do, and the bunk beds/mattresses for the boys... they were relatively new!

I had known for few months that I'd have to leave... I think it's around July that I finally came to that epiphany after many years of indecision. I'd want to believe that the man also knew that this was inevitable, or maybe not, as he'd like to project the image of a home in order! The marriage had been problematic from the onset and it's finally come to a halt, we had hardly spoken or had any meaningful conversation in four years and we had not shared the same room or bed for the same length of time. Even though it took me almost thirteen years to make up my mind, but as soon as I did, I started to think about the logistics and making plans.

I hunted for a rented accommodation in the same neighbourhood. It was one of my friends who first saw the property on Gumtree and thought it might just be what I needed! It was! Our packed suitcases had always been on standby! I wanted to soften the impacts on the kids as best as possible. Living in the same locality would be easier on them, moving to a similar accommodation would be familiar, not having to change schools, childminders and Family Doctor/GP etc. But the most important thing was that I wanted as little drama as possible. He loved his kids, even though he was unable to factor their wellbeing and welfare into his everyday plans… even though he was unable to create time for them, or make sacrifices or be inconvenienced for their sakes. With all plans in place, it was just a matter of time or when. It was hard to book a removal van when I didn't know the exact day/time that I'd leave but I had numbers for different companies. As nature would have it, I spotted a removal van as I was picking up the kids from the childminder on that last day. Two men were sitting inside and they seemed to be chatting off idly. I approached them and asked if they were available for work, one of them said, "Give us the address and give us three-four hours." And that was it!

We stood in front of the house with all our suitcases. The removal men were putting the boys' bunk bed and two mattresses in the vehicle. They created a space for the suitcases. I cast a last look at the house that we had lived for nine years of the thirteen-year marriage! I put a lengthy note through the letter box for him as he was away and also the keys to the house. My daughter held the younger boy whilst I held the older. We entered into the car that was waiting for us and travelled ahead whilst the van followed us... It was like travelling into the unknown...it was actually travelling into the unknown! Ashamed, disgraced and metaphorically stripped, I found myself alone with three kids at 41 years old, starting all over again!

The new address was a few streets away... it was within the same neighbourhood that we had lived but it felt totally different and strange! It was an accommodation that I had rented a month earlier and the one I had visited a few times with the kids before we finally moved! As we started and continued our new lives in this new place, I daily remembered the music that was playing on a TV channel when I first came to sign the tenancy agreement with the landlords... It was Bounce by Calvin Harris... it was kind of proverbial in relation to my particular circumstances as all I needed was a bounce... A spring in my steps... looked like it was going to be a long journey but one that would certainly bring me back home... to life!

Chapter 1
The Crash – A Bang Long Coming!

It's been nine years since my marriage finally came to a halt! The children have grown. The twelve-year-old is now twenty-one; the nine-year-old, eighteen, and the six-year-old, fifteen! They seem to be doing well in their own different ways but I cannot stop wondering if they have been able to escape emotionally unscathed from all this turmoil. I am now fifty years old! I want to believe that I have grown not only in age but in grace and character too. As I continue to find my ways through life and juggling my differing roles; I have found that some days are better than the others. Some days I seem to have a lot of energy, on other days, it's so tough that I feel so overwhelmed that it seems I'd crumble under the weight/pressure of my life's demands! Some days I'm grateful for being alive and sometimes I do moan! But I have found that I seem to regain my strength and be more inspired when I'm thankful… when I choose to remember how far the children and I have come… when I cast my mind back to when I was still actually down in the rubbles…when I appreciate that it could have been worse… when I'm grateful for the grace that I have been freely given by God! And the strength to keep on going.

My crash was not sudden but gradual, but with a bang and severe impacts nonetheless! The proverbial hand writing had been on the wall for the thirteen-year life span of the marriage! I would even confess that there had been some red flags prior to the marriage, even though these were not significantly pronounced until I was in the marriage – these, I naively thought, love would conquer! Well, this happened not to be the case. The relationship did not improve but became seriously dysfunctional with each passing day. I was determined to hold on; I was prepared to, come what may! It never occurred to me that I could leave my marriage one day. I resigned myself and my situation to fate! I laboured and laboured! Carrying the responsibilities that the two people in a marriage should have shared.

Many people thought I was a single parent whilst still married! I was approached by a woman in a previous neighbourhood about support single parents. She gave me information leaflets to signpost me to some organisations. I thanked her but said that I was married. She was shocked but apologised. She said she had observed my running around for few years and genuinely thought that I was single and might need help!

With the passing of time, I became a shell of my old self, to the point that I no longer was in sync with who I was. My mother, who visited from abroad, did not even recognise me at first sight! My reality became blurred and I nearly lost my mind. Juggling my roles as a wife, mother, carer and employee within a seriously dysfunctional and unsupportive relationship took everything in me. I was nearly wiped out! I was running on auto pilot!

But who would have believed the story of my struggles? We looked like your regular everyday family. Some who had no privy information had sadly called it an enviable family and marriage in the past! The wife, the husband and the three kids! Living in the big house at the end of the street! Going to church on Sundays in a nice car! The man was neither openly brash nor brutish! A solemn and reserved guy to the outsiders... a cool dude! But only I and few people very close to me knew what was happening behind the shut door! Two previous acquittances who were single would regularly say to me that "at least you're married", each time we were discussing life and its issues.

My struggles were not so obvious to many. Or it could be that they knew but were unsure or unwilling to become involved. Most of the time, these issues are termed family matters! They were ingrained issues like overt and covert manipulation and control; lies, deceptions and facades; cheating, exploitation and abuse; lack of appreciation and approval; denial; insensitivity and arrogance; using sex deprivation as a weapon; unfairness and hiding behind religion to pervert justice, equity and humanity; gender roles demarcation within the marriage (he would assert himself as a patriarch when it suited him but not when he needed my money!); some destructive principles such as: "It's a man's world", "we are not the same",... "You are a woman", "do as I say, not as I do" or, "It's the duty of a woman to make her marriage work", or "women should be submissive to men" (even when he had seriously disrespected me and had not demonstrated love and compassion towards me as his wife as instructed in the Bible) etc. He conducted his affairs as though he was a bachelor... without thinking about the effects of his decisions on others within the family. He carried on as though he had no responsibilities towards his wife and kids. He preferred to be unburdened physically, financially, domestically, emotionally, child-care wise, etc. He 'travelled very light'. He could not afford to be inconvenienced as he pursued what he believed were his goals and ambitions at the expense of the happiness and wellbeing of his wife and, by extension, his kids.

Everything about me was controlled! How I dressed and groomed myself! Who I talked to! Where I went! Contacts and relationships with family and friends! My hopes and aspirations! I could not express myself in ways that I liked or was familiar with. I lost my identity and individuality! I lost my voice! I was silenced by force... my light became seriously dimmed so that my man could shine at all costs! I was gradually repackaged and redesigned! I was overwhelmed, overworked and disrespected in my marriage. I felt lonely and unloved! The environment and the relationship did not foster any harmony within me. My consciousness was broken into pieces. It was by the grace of God that I pulled through and am still standing!

I was not involved in any decision in my marriage, even the ones involving the money that I worked for! None of the bills were in my name, even though I paid for almost all the bills in my home for thirteen years! Everything had to be in my man's name, including the mortgage. That made him feel like a 'real man' who's in control of his home and his woman, even at the expense of my toil, sweat and blood! It was like being a slave in the 21st Century. The trauma was immense.

Time and time again, I have heard people say, "No marriage is perfect… every marriage has challenges." Yes, of course. Challenges abound in marriages. They are circumstances that you cannot readily predict. People may not be able to project that their children or spouses would encounter illness/disability, that they would lose their jobs or have their houses repossessed, etc. Those are the challenges of marriages. But from my experiences, people should know and understand the fundamentals of relationships and should be certain to a great degree that these are available in their relationships and marriages. They should possess the level of self-identity that can filter through these issues without ignoring red flags. Mutual interest, love, respect, care, understanding, sensitivity, trust and sacrifice should be the core and fundamental blocks of any marriage, if that marriage is to be meaningful and functional. So, from my personal experiences, it's about the obvious fundamentals and not necessarily the unforeseen challenges!

When I do get down to it, I do strongly pity the man. It's hard for me to understand how he could be neglecting of his significant relationships whilst pursuing goals that he felt would give him the status and accomplishment he so desperately wanted. What more could be fulfilling than ensuring the wellbeing of your family, regardless of the sacrifice (physically, mentally, emotionally, practically, financially etc.) it required. Seeing your family as your priority is the best achievement anyone can make! I still wonder how he got his priorities so messed up. I wanted to believe that he's not a terrible person. Sometimes I do wonder whether he's aware and understanding of these issues, whether they were intentional, whether they were due to pain from any of his previous experiences, whether he genuinely lacked self-awareness and emotional intelligence, whether they were due to his upbringing, etc. But the facts that he chose to be in denial, disregarded any expressed concerns and refused to foster meaningful communication made situations the more difficult. He was not determined to work on the marriage at all. It didn't look as though it was a priority! He had stated that it was the duty of a woman to make 'her marriage' work. He was busy pursuing different businesses that brought no dividends... draining and wasting the resources that were supposed to be invested in his kids' future and unilaterally making all these decisions. He was the man of the house! He's the only man I know that would wake up in the morning, sorted himself out and left the house or mentioned that he's travelling for six to eight weeks, a day before without giving any consideration to his children's' care and wellbeing. He had very minimal involvement in childcare, whether financially, practically, emotionally. Even when his office used to be only a five-minute drive from home and he was working for himself, he could not participate in childcare. I still had to pay through my nose!

One of the children started to display the signs of disability and autism around the age of two. It was another blow to an existing rocky marriage. Caring for a child with disability takes everything in you! To him, it was easier to go into denial than to accept that there was a problem. It was a way of dealing with his pain and avoiding taking responsibilities. At least if you denied, you wouldn't have to do anything, but if you accepted, there would be lots to do and it'd require your all. He has been very minimally involved with this child and his circumstances. At the early stage, he said, "There's nothing wrong with my son… he's just shy… he'll outgrow it." The child is now eighteen years old. He hasn't outgrown autism! A lot has happened in the last sixteen years since he first showed signs. The father was not involved in any significant way in any of the processes from various appointments and testing for diagnosis, to educational decisions, to children and adult social services, to managing day to day behaviours, safety issues, future, impact on his siblings etc. Nothing; this man dissociated himself completely! Maybe he genuinely thought by doing that, he'd wake up one day and the autism would have disappeared. He met with the children twice in 2019, after having not seeing them for three years. In one of the meetings, he asked me if our child with special needs (who has required round the clock care because of the severity of his disability) would eventually start to live independently on his own one day! That's what he wanted to see happen, that's why he'd buried his head in the sand. He'd never dirtied his hands or been inconvenienced in relation to this child or any of the other children! He refused to be involved in any way and by so doing, missed out on what it means to be a real father! But sadly enough, he was not seeing it this way… he arrogantly convinced himself that he was in his children's lives even though he knew nothing about them or their journey so far!

When I asked him if he genuinely believes, from looking at this child, that he can live independently, he could not answer. When I said he'd continue use to require support and care from other people and would require supported living accommodation in future, he asked me if that's what the professionals have said! He had always refused to acknowledge my knowledge or views in this area even though

I have looked after this child for eighteen years and I also do a similar thing in my daytime job. I said to him that I do not need a professional to tell me as I am not only a professional in similar field, who contributes significantly to the decisions about the functioning and living plans for vulnerable individuals, I'm also this child's parent. I know him like the back of my hand and I have been involved in every aspect of his life and disability since birth. He kept quiet and could not utter a word!

Anyhow, sorry to go off tangent! You are probably wondering, at this stage, why I did not leave this marriage sooner. Yes, you are right. I should have left a long time ago, but I was incarcerated by religion, culture, other people's opinions, family and friends and particularly how leaving would affect our children. My own fear also played into the equation – I did not want to become a single parent! It's against my cultural upbringing. There is hardly any respect for unmarried women, especially unmarried mothers in my culture! African culture, in addition to religion, put massive responsibilities on a woman within a marriage at expensive costs to her life and sanity! Most girls were raised to become submissive wives but sadly not many boys were raised to become responsible husbands! I thought I couldn't leave because of all these reasons, but towards the end, I found stronger reasons to leave such as that the children needed to be raised with calmness and clarity of mind in a love-filled environment; they should be raised to have the understanding of a functional and meaningful relationship between a man and a woman; they should be raised to understand how loving marriages should and could be, regardless of challenges; I could go mad; I could break down physically (my BP has been hitting the roof from the age of 30!); I could become homeless (Bailiff attended the old house twice within eighteen months, period, as he'd repeatedly re-mortgaged the house); I could attack this man out of frustrations and potentially became a criminal! Yes, these reasons were stronger and enough for me. By the time I had found the strength to pull and put myself together, I walked out of my marriage at the age of forty-one, with three children (one with severe learning disability) and our suitcases! Nothing more, nothing less! I literally did not know where I was going as I was unsure and still unsure of what the future held but interestingly enough, my emotion at leaving was more of a relief than bitterness, despite everything. I rationalised it as a possible opportunity to have another chance at life… of possibly experiencing wellbeing and especially harmony within myself again… my beings and elements coming together in a wholesome manner!

Chapter 2
Sorting Through the Rubbles – Finding the Pieces!

I sometimes wondered how he must have felt when he realised that we had left home… when he read through the letter that I'd left for him… The shock or possibly the pain that he must have passed through, that must have been enormous. Regardless of how obvious the problems of a marriage are, no man wants to be seeing as having failed in being able to hold his family together. It must have been a big slap, especially on someone like him who liked to project an image of a man in control of his family. It's like the facade and mask were shattered. Poor man!

As a sort of damage control of his shattered image, he went on a rampage! He went from person to person to tell different stories and all these were to assassinate my character. They were very damaging stories. Some people challenged and confronted him, some people felt indifferent whilst some seemed to have gone along with him. Whilst doing this, he was also asking some of them to persuade me not to leave the house. He said he'd like me to continue to pay the mortgage as he didn't want to lose the property. He said he was planning to relocate abroad and would be visiting the United Kingdom from time to time and would eventually transfer the mortgage to my name in future! A particular female pastor asked him how he expected me to cope with all these responsibilities; he reportedly told the woman that I'd cope because I had a good job! The woman was very upset, she stated that she saw no empathy, no love, no care! She asked him to leave!

What I found strange with his strategies was that he could actually approach so many people about his collapsed marriage whilst he had adamantly refused for thirteen years to approach these same people to mediate and potentially help to resolve our mounting issues and possibly salvage the marriage. He had also strictly forbidden me from bringing a third party into a marriage that we had both failed to make work. Also, I found it strange, just like some of the people he approached, that he was very interested in salvaging the property, more than he was about the marriage. They said he never once demonstrated any willingness to rescue his marriage, but only his name, reputation and property!

As painful and ridiculous as the entire smear campaigns were, I chose to handle them differently. All I wanted to find was calmness and peace to sift through the mess. I did not want to be dragged into the same issues that I had contended with for thirteen years! I was not interested in retaliating or defending myself. Despite our relationship having failed to work, he was still the father of my children and they loved him, and from early on, I wanted to respect them by not engaging in damaging their father whether with them or before other people.

He made his first contact twelve weeks after we left, via an e mail to our daughter when he could have called my mobile/cell phone to speak to his children, even if he didn't want to talk to me. The mail was a nasty one that got the girl and myself upset. She replied but he did not respond. I mailed him to encourage him to be an adult and to liaise with me directly rather than attempting to aggravate me via the children. I said we should at least be civil to each other because of the children and that if he chose to continue with his strategy, I would block his mail and phone accesses and he would not be able to get through to any of us except if he went to court to apply for child's visitation or custody. He stopped sending nasty mails!

The first time he spoke to me or the children was six months after we left. He said he'd like to see his children. He saw them face to face at a public place for the first time a week later. He has been seeing them at an average of one time in twelve to eighteen months, a total of about six to seven face-to-face meetings in nine years! He speaks to them on the phone once in eight to twelve weeks! I have never for once stopped him from making these contacts, as patchy and as inconsistent as they are. Even though the contacts make no significant difference to our lives, I do recognise that they are emotionally helpful to both the children and him. He has moved on with his life and has been in a relationship since day one. I have always wished him all happiness.

Back to the children and I… Here we are now. I'm trying to assess and sift through the damage. To identify what had been lost, destroyed, what can be rescued and what had remained wholesome, valuable and intact. I needed to know what we had to work with. On the surface of it, it did look like everything I worked for and believed in seemed to have been lost marriage/growing old together, raising my children within marriage, house/investment, home, status, respect etc. It did look like I lost almost everything that I had laboured for; I was alone, lonely, stressed, stripped naked and abandoned. But on a deep reflection as a believer, I had and still have a lot to be grateful for.... given what I went through I was blessed to be alive and sane! I have a lot of good to hold onto. I have had to keep on reminding myself of these everyday:

- I know, have and serve God
- My children and I are still alive, standing and healthy. They are doing well in their own ways and in their education.
- My child with SEN is manageable, by the grace of God, despite everyday challenges.
- I am fit enough to parent my children despite all the pain and stress.
- I have good education that allows me to continue to explore information, options and opportunities.
- Fit enough to practice my profession and have a job that allows me to have some level of income to look after my children and myself.
- Even though I lost my house (the house had seriously fallen into a negative equity by the time I left), I have a roof over my head in terms of a rented accommodation.
- I have good and encouraging people around me.
- Still engaging in charity work from time to time.

- I'm open minded and willing to do more meaningful things. I want to keep on working on myself and continue to build on my character.

Chapter 3
Getting Up and Looking Up – The Sun Still Shines! (Carrying My Baggage with Acceptance!)

I started to get up from the rubbles; shaking off the dust. Carried stuffs that had the potentials to be salvaged. Started to take steps to forge ahead whilst attempting to swallow my sense of failing and shame. And to manage my fear and anxiety. I realised very early on that there was a need for me to come to a total acceptance of my situation… to not allow shame and fear to lead to any pretence or colouring of my situations in different lights. I have got to own my issues with no apologies. Very important!

The first few weeks in the new house were strange. Even though we were still in the same neighbourhood, but it was still different, nonetheless. A different street… new neighbours… unfamiliar routes to the bus stops… having a massive river just minutes from our front door… a primary school nearby… and the business of school rush hours … there were a lot of things to get used to. But despite these… having to explore the new house and become used to it was fun in itself but not necessarily to everyone. My child with special needs has hardly gone one week without mentioning the old house... even after nine years! He associates the old house to having his dad... it was a place where he had certain toys that he no longer has... it was a place where certain childminders/carers looked after him... it was the place where he remembered few neighbours and their kids... it was essentially the place of his childhood ... from birth to age nine! He hasn't forgotten... he probably never would... when he was upset about anything, he'd say that he wanted to return to the old house, even though he was aware that his dad no longer lives there too... changes are hard for most people, but in particular for Individuals with autism and learning disability.

We also started experiencing other major changes that were more demanding as well, the following month after moving house. A lot seemed to have happened within short periods apart and these seemed very impacting to nearly all of us. My child's mainstream school decided that his special education needs would be better met in a specialist unit... this new unit was a bit of travel and in a totally different locality and a significant change given that he's always been able to get to school within ten to fifteen minutes. Just as we were attempting to find ways to manage... his minder/carer of many years was moving houses too. So, this child would begin to go to his minder in a new house... who in turn would support him to get to his new school! A lot of changes within a short time!

This same month, I started a new job... with the same company I have always worked for but in a totally different setting... this new setting was near home which made my juggling a bit manageable. Have I mentioned that we had to change church as well? Yes, we did... it was essential that we did, given that our church wasn't the type that was accepting of separation/divorce and the pressure and interference was becoming a bit stressful.

In the midst of all this, settling the kids down in the new house, raising them as a single parent, whilst carrying on with my job and caring role were my utmost priorities! But underlying was the massive fear of how I was going to successfully achieve all this, especially raising children that were not badly affected by the failed relationship and absent father. It was very apparent, right from the onset that my ex was not likely to be significantly involved with the care and upbringing of the kids. He wasn't to any meaningful extent whilst we were under the same roof, and he made his first contact twelve weeks after the separation... not to ask after his kids but to cast aspersions... he asked to see his kids almost five months after we separated even though we were living in the same city.

Like I was saying... I was bugged down with these massive fears that I couldn't shake off. How was I going to cope with raising three kids on my own and having a job? The complexities of looking after children and their needs alone, navigating school processes, admissions to colleges and university form completions, referring to yourself as Ms and the impact on your and your children's chances and prospects etc. Would I break down physically, or mentally, or both? Would I be deemed unfit to parent or to hold down a job? How was I going to cope with being a care provider for my child on an ongoing basis? The autism and learning disability are not changing... they have continued to impact every aspect of his and our lives. Would I be able to give my children a decent life on my current income? I lost my home and my house... would I be able to have another mortgage/investment that could guarantee my kids' future financial security?

My biggest fears and worries seemed to have centred on raising emotionally stable and grounded children who were not seriously affected by not having their father in their lives! Every child wants to be reassured by the love, presence and the guidance of their fathers. Also troubling for me was becoming a sort of statistic 'single parent', facing the rejection and disappointment of a failed marriage. The loss of marital status and the dignity and respect that normally come with it, especially from my culture. A woman is most times not seen as dignified and respectable without a marriage... it's even worse for a divorced woman! What would be the impact of this status on my children? Being raised by a single parent, especially by a woman, is most times not seen as having the potential to yield a positive outcome... it's more like there is an unwritten expectations for children raised outside of marriage to fall by the way sides? To be deprived socially, emotionally, financially, educationally etc. And particularly to be unable to hold down meaningful relationships themselves... it's a case of 'like father, like son, like mother, like daughter'. Becoming a statistic – my worse fear – divorced, loss of status, single parenthood, complexities of looking after children and their needs alone, navigating school processes, admissions to college and university form completions, referring to yourself as Ms and the impact on your and your children's chances and prospects etc.

One other nagging fear is about myself... Would I be able to establish a meaningful and functional relationship like I have always wanted to? Would I be able to attract a man at my age and with my baggage? It's a lot easier when I married in my twenties etc. Would I grow old alone? How would I manage my loneliness? Would I ever be able to have a life separate from working and raising children?

I have always been a worrier. Even though I was petrified with my fears... I also had first-hand knowledge about how this could disable me, if not adequately managed. I have stuff to deal with! I needed to Identify what I could control, influence, or what I had to accept. I needed to face my fears and do it afraid, if that's what it took. And that's what I did! Devising working strategies that were practical and realistic... putting my and kids' emotional wellbeing at the heart of all issues... finding peace... finding calmness. I remembered having to buy a light green, CALM ceramic, as a daily visual prompt of my determination to approach; all I need to do with peace and calm.

I identified what I was possibly unable to salvage/rescue. I have had to accept these fears and shame that I have been mostly afraid of. I have come to realise that attempting to prevent these issues or colouring them otherwise are the very reasons most people (men and women) are unable to leave dysfunctional relationships and marriages that have the potential to endanger their body and mind. In my situation, I was held back for many years whilst gradually losing my being because I was so much concerned with the Church's view on separation and divorce, how my church and cultural communities would perceive me, how some of my friends and families would view my decision, impact of divorce on my children's mental/emotional and general wellbeing. But over the years, the only one of these concerns that has been most meaningful has been to support my children as optimally as possible, from being emotionally affected by the break-up, I can't be bothered with the other concerns… I am not prepared to continue to please people and ask for their approval and validations about issues to do with my life. I'm done with that!

Chapter 4
Restructuring and Regrouping

I started to do it afraid! Otherwise I wouldn't be able to forge ahead. But to tell the truth, the grass is not always greener at the other side, though it may appear so sometimes. The ideal setting to raise children is within a marital relationship. Living and raising children as a single parent is not easy, especially for women! It's the one that comes with a lot of complexities and should be navigated carefully. However, there comes a time when being on oneself is far better than being in a destructive and dysfunctional marriage. In relation to marriages, the Bible says that two heads are better than one and also that iron sharpens iron. But sadly, these wonderful and Godly ethos have not worked in my own marriage and in so many Christian marriages. As a result, I do believe that it's possible for a woman to raise functional children on her own, despite how difficult it is, but such can only happen with resources, especially finances, and particularly a good level of emotional stability. The woman must be mentally and emotionally stable, very important ingredients! She must be strong, determined and resilient! And be prepared to find peace with God, with herself and with other people.

I had been very stressed for many years within the marriage, even though I continued to function optimally. Sometimes, when I look back, I wonder how I had survived if not for God! It was like running on auto pilot! My job was not lagging, and I think it was because of my field of work, I knew the triggers to be aware of. I kept on reminding myself that I should not break down. I couldn't afford to break down. I had to be fit to raise my children. I had to be fit to practice my profession! But then, I knew that there was so far that I could actually push this. By the time I left the marriage, I was really spent out; I had been deprived of my substances. I was very tired, overwhelmed, wearied, lonely and unsure of my future. Not only was I spent emotionally and mentally, I was also wasted physically. I had gone from my regular UK size twelve to around size eight. Even though people around me and at work were envying my size, I did recognise that it was not a healthy weight loss, my muscles and skin weren't firm and toned. It's was a weight loss caused by excessive stress, sleeplessness and loss of appetite. I was wasting away! I'd come to weight loss and physical health later. Now back to my emotions!

As I started looking into the issues at hand and the obvious challenges of singlehood in addition to my existing roles as a mother, a carer and an employee: I was acutely aware that I needed to work on my frail emotions if I was to be able to manage my life's pressure, moving forward, especially with regards to raising balanced children. I needed to heal emotionally and to replenish. Finding and sustaining inner peace and harmony became my number one priority! To help myself in this area, I turned upward and inward. I have had to adopt different strategies like the ones below:

Solitude and Reflection

For the first two years, I kept a low profile. From most friends and family members who would tell me that it was wrong to leave my marriage. From the Church members and Pastors who would remind me of eternal damnation. From cultural and local associates who would frown on single parenthood. I changed Church. I did not discuss with most people around me, including my mother who was abroad. I never told her for almost two years that I'd left my marriage even though we talked weekly. When she'd ask to speak to him, I'd say he was not available. She assumed he was doing shift works and not always available at home. She wouldn't have been able to handle the truth initially; she couldn't accept it after nine years! It's one particular heart-break she was unable to get over even in her last days. It's uncommon, or shall I say unacceptable, for an African woman to leave her marriage! African girls (especially of my generation and the ones before me) were raised to be mothers and wives... obedient and submissive wives, regardless of what their marital experiences were! They were expected to remain in their marriages, come what may, for their children's sake. It's a general saying that the children are the rewards of the married woman! My failed marriage was a great shame on my mother in particular! It affected her greatly. Even as she became very frail and mentally incoherent, she'd from time to time ask me to 'greet my husband'. She refused to accept my single status!

Anyhow, I kept a low profile and turned inward like I was saying. I used every available time and space to go into reflection and solitude. I had a lot of opportunities to reflect on how I had made my choices in life and how I had ended up where I was. I considered factors that were beyond my control. I looked myself very hard in the face about factors that I was responsible for. How had I failed myself or marriage; it's not always completely another person's fault. We were in it together. Without taking my own share of responsibilities, I'd make similar errors in decision making in the future, I've got to be a better person!

Seeking God through Prayers and His Words

At the core of my being is my personal relationship with God. I am a believer! My spirituality has been my anchor. As a result, I have ascribed the totality of my being into God's hands even though I do recognise that I have a part to play and certain areas to control as far as my destiny is concerned. I will do what I can. But, overall, I have surrendered to God what I have no control over. It gives me a sense of peace.

Regular devotion and prayers are very crucial to my and family's wellbeing. I engage the children as much as possible, but optimally, it's mostly me standing in the gap for my family. Having the regular private and quiet times to read my Bible and other related books, listening to audio messages or watching videos and praying are probably the major instruments fostering my healing!

Using all other available Resources to aid Healing

My peculiar personality has meant that I need to be on my own from time to time in the house. Away from my regular tasks and from my kids to reflect and replenish physically and mentally. Having to do this can be tricky when you have kids and especially one with a disability. But over the years, I have repeatedly explained to my children the importance of having my personal space. They have come to accept and become used to this, especially as they were growing up and understanding better. It became a habit and a routine. They knew mummy needed to rest, sleep, pray, listen to messages and would not like to be disturbed in those short periods.

I have always been an ardent reader. I bought a lot of books of different subjects relevant to my circumstances. Biographies, Memoirs, Self-help books, etc. I also bought books that were mostly fictional just to relax and chill out sometimes. I have had to do this as my default position has been to be very focussed and serious minded… I have always realised that I needed to be able to engage in light and fun pursuits from time to time.

Using technology, especially devices with accesses to YouTube has also been very fundamental to my wellbeing. Listening to music or singing along to these has been very therapeutic for me. Listening to the experiences of other people on YouTube has also helped me a lot. I have clocked hundreds of hours of motivational and inspirational videos in managing emotions, relationships, building boundaries, self-awareness, identity and confidence, raising kids, emotional intelligence and other skills for living.

I have always been able to look myself in the face… to be objective in relation to my circumstances. I know where my strength and areas requiring improvement lie. I am very familiar with emotions that can impact negatively on me and my kids' wellbeing. Right from the onset, I started to explore my emotions… rebuilding walks and boundaries…

evaluating and redefining my values... putting peace and serenity at the core of my values and amplifying others such as autonomy (my voice, my choice); authenticity (being myself), mutual respect, honesty and integrity, responsibility, freedom and independence, kindness and empathy and HOPE. There were other ethos that have also helped me to heal, such as knowing my limits, live and let's live (placing no expectations on others) and living within my means. My children helped me to heal as I needed to be reasonably grounded and stable to look after them.

I started to work on my fear of rejection and loneliness. I started to look at the issues such as do men still find me attractive. Dating in my forties/fifties was difficult than in my twenties... Dating complicated by my baggage etc. There are tendencies for these internal conflicts to cause frustrations that can lead to poor choices and decision making. I made a couple of those choices over the nine years, based on fear, but came back to my senses quickly. They were not necessarily bad guys but they were not right for me. I have got to do better and learn from my mistakes. I'm managing my years of singleness, concentrating mostly on improving myself and being the kind of person I would love to attract and date – working through my emotions, character, my career, my finances, values and goals, fostering a better self-identity and individuality, looking after children and helping them to find their feet in life, etc. As I continued to move on and focus on what I need to do, I started to become better in myself. I started to seek a closure. I put in a divorce petition five years after separation. That's a totally different story for another day.

Talking to Others

Talking to others from time to time has been crucial. I have had to structure this task as I do not always have a lot of time to engage in talking. But I have devised means of ensuring this, for example, using my commuting time, because I do realise how useful it can be, not only for me but for other family and friends, especially as the COVID lockdowns have meant that people need to make social and emotional connections with others. At the initial years, whilst trying to find my feet, a lot of friends dedicated their time and other resources to ensure that they talked to me regularly, prayed for me and encouraged me. Of this, I am most grateful.

Walking and Jogging

Physically exercising has also helped me to heal to a good extent. The hormone released via exercise can foster relaxation and calmness. Open space, fresh air on one's face, reflection, time to one's self, etc. are all very healthy. I make sure that I walk every day and jog from time to time.

Writing and Journaling

I have always loved to write, even as a ten-year-old girl. I kept diaries for many years and notebooks or pieces of papers. I have to write! But due to advancement in technology, I now mostly journal on my mobile phone. Being able to journal frees and de-clutters my mind of emotive materials. I knew I had healed and moved on when I returned to old notes and couldn't believe I wrote them in the first place! When I said, "Oh my God... did I actually write that?"... then I'd know I'm sorted on that subject, at least for that period.

Employment:

My day job is a major factor in my healing process. I have never actually stopped working (except when on maternity leave and once on a three-week sick leave) despite the complexities of my personal live. I have continued to work through the difficult marriage, despite my child's disability and all the complications and even when the marriage came to a final halt! To be honest, it's not as though it's never crossed my mind to stop working. It has on a few occasions. Not only because of my personal life's demands but also because my job itself is a seriously challenging one at the best of times but very fulfilling! But I never gave in to this thought because I have, for the longest time, realised how important working is for me and my family. It's one way of not been consumed by my personal palaver.

The relationship between my personal and professional lives is what can be described as a symbiosis. They rely on each other for their very existence! Working to me is not just about generating an income but it's also to do with generating life and wellbeing for me and my children! Work helps to distract me from my everyday personal issues. It provides purpose and focus in a different direction. It gives me the drive to get up from that bed and that room. To meet and work with others. To use my experience to serve others. To get fresh air on my face and smell the rose. Work gives me the opportunity to engage my mind creatively and purposefully. It boosts my overall wellbeing and that of my children. Without my job, I would have been totally consumed by my own pain and struggles. I'm so blessed to continue to be fit to raise my children!

As much as my work benefits my personal life; my personal life also fosters my work positively and significantly. My personal experiences help me to approach my job with more compassion and commitment. It helps me to care for the vulnerable people with more understanding and in non-judgemental manner. My knowledge of and encounter with different organisations and their processes over the years in relation to my child's disability have been very useful to my work. I do not only approach my work as a professional but also as a parent/carer of a child with disability. I wear two hats instead of one! I can understand the pain, struggles, loss, fear, hope and aspirations of the parents/families of the vulnerable individuals who I care for. It gives me broader perspectives as I continue to practice my profession!

I have been blessed to have a circle of paid childminders that have assisted over the years, especially related to my child with disability. Even though I have always been able to get him ready for school in the mornings, I have required the support of a number of childminders to collect him from the school transport and engage with him until I return home in the evening. Without these wonderful people, I wouldn't have been able to handle everything by myself. I am forever grateful! Over the years, they have become like family members, checking on us, offering to assist if I need to go out with friends as they realise that it's very important that I socialise from time to time as respites from my family and work lives!

Chapter 5
Watering and Raising My Seeds – Fostering the Children

If there was something that I was so frightened about after the crash, it was the terrible fear that I might not be able to raise emotionally healthy children... ones unaffected by a broken home and single parenthood... I was and still am constantly worried about the impacts of this terrible tragedy on my children... it is indeed a great tragedy, especially on children, when a home is broken. Every child wants their parents together... regardless of what's happening between the adults involved. They want that unit... that home.

Easing the impacts of the crash in whatever ways I can and helping the children to heal has been my number one priority right from the beginning. It's one of the reasons I did not move too far away from the old address... and also the reason I moved to a house similar to the one we previously had. To maintain some level of sameness and minimise the changes that could make the crash too difficult to bear. They still attended the same schools, had the same family doctor, same child-minder (nanny), shopped at the same stores, lived in the same locality and post code and accessed the same facilities they were familiar with. Meanwhile, as much as I tried to control some of these variables, some changes occurred that I could not influence, such as the nanny changing address few weeks after our address changed, my child with disability was transferred to a special education need school a few weeks after the crash and we changed church due to pressure gradually mounting in our old church regarding the crash. All these extra changes brought with them certain challenges of their own but I was determined to help the children settle and start to heal and get used to our new lives. Positively fostering them has been the biggest desire that I hold.

Reconnecting with my children one on one and as a group was what I started to do as we began to settle down... as the dust of the rubbles started to settle. I did not want to assume that I knew the extents of the impacts of a broken home on them; I wanted them to start to express their individual views. Just when I was thinking about how to navigate these issues, two of the children started to talk to their teachers at their separate schools about how they would have wanted their parents to be together. And how sad they were that their parents could not make it work. The schools invited me to meetings. Even though they were different schools, the views were the same. The schools and I acknowledged the children's concerns but explained that adult relationships were sometimes complicated. That it was sometimes better for adults to separate if the relationship was no longer healthy and that they can become healthy in their own separate lives and continue to love their children as individuals rather than as a couple. I explained to them that sometimes children can grow and lead functional lives with one parent contrary to the old beliefs that they are better off within a couple relationship /marriage at all costs regardless of how dysfunctional the marriage has become.

The schools asked them what they thought could be useful to them moving forward. They said they'd want me to spend one on one time with them in their own preferred activities in addition to our family/group activities. They felt one to one interaction would allow them to express themselves better. They also requested for occasional family meetings. They'd want their dad to call them regularly... the school wanted me to ask their dad to call them... but to tell you the truth... I struggled with this assignment... I did not believe it was my duty to tell a dad to call his children! A dad should want to speak with his children without being prompted for God's sake!

Even though I had a major issue with having to remind my ex to call or interact with his children, it had been my plan right from the beginning to foster interactions between him and the children whenever he decided to speak with them or see them. I have never at any time attempted to block interactions. I believe it's emotionally healthy, especially for the children.

I started to engage in one to one sessions with the children. We've largely done stuffs together as a group in our old lives. Mother and daughter-spa, cake and custard shops, going for walks, football sessions, cooking sessions, going for meals... opportunities to talk and explore emotions in fun and less structured ways. Watching favourite TV programmes as mummy and daughter or mummy and sons and using the opportunities to find out how/what they are feeling. We hold family meetings every two to three months to check our individual and family progress.

Helping the children to explore emotions, identity and values are the main objectives of fostering their positive growth. I bought books for them on various subjects and encouraged them to read in order to learn from the experiences of other people and broaden their mind. I bought books written by their favourite celebrities (especially the ones raised by single parents) on how they have overcome difficulties. They heard stories of hope by exploring the lives of great people that have been raised outside of the traditional family settings such Barack Obama, Anthony Joshua, Oprah Winfrey, Lewis Hamilton etc. Over time, the children grew to love literature to a very great extent that two of them joined literacy groups in schools, one is an ardent writer that had been recognised by a local author and one is regularly holding book reviews on Instagram.

Story time is another way that I have adopted to connect to the children on an emotional level. Sharing my childhood upbringing and life's experiences with them (the good, the bad and the ugly), giving them the opportunities to ask questions, being authentic about my flaws, comparing my experiences to theirs as people born and raised in millennial era and finding common grounds despite how different our eras are.

Finding joy in the little everyday events are one of the ways we connect as a family – going for walks, meals, cooking sessions, picnics, watching their favourite programmes with them, cinemas, meeting their friends, mother and daughter sessions, mother and son sessions, etc. We watch different television programmes/YouTube videos together and share our views and perspectives. We have favourite joint family programs such as Football, Hell Kitchen/Kitchen Nightmares, Super Nanny, My Wife and Kids, What Would You Do? Extreme Cheap-stakes, Madea Series etc. I also share links to a lot of self-development videos/courses related to skills' building, personal growth, being raised by a single parent, absentee father ('father wound'), confidence and self-esteem, holding your place in the world, etc. Travels also helped the children to explore the world and experience other people's cultures.

In as much as I have been liberal and accommodating of my kids' needs, I have always known how important it'd be to also establish boundaries that can foster them positively. These are mainly to do with personal and domestic goal settings, meeting their educational deadlines, completing what they have agreed to do, purposeful and constructive friendships, expectations regarding visits by friends or when they have to visit friends, attendances at events and personal boundaries and discipline. I have endeavoured to put my own needs on hold to a very significant extent to support and protect them and also to assist them to learn the importance of self-discipline. I have wanted to make the way I live my life a message to them whilst they begin to navigate their own paths.

The children are growing into responsible adults, thanks to God. They are works in progress. There are areas in which I'm fully satisfied and reassured and there are still few areas that I have continued to monitor. I bring these areas up with them from time to time to get and understand their own perspectives. This COVID season has greatly impacted them in different ways like the rest of the world, especially to do with changes to their educational, social and community engagements. It's my hope that the children will grow up and be able to hold their individual places in this world that is ever changing. I pray they will be able to use the varieties of positive and constructive tools available to them to become better people and to make positive contributions to their society. As a parent, I do hope that a day will come when I'm fully reassured and rested knowing that my children are, or will be, OK.

Chapter 6
The Voices of Hope

I have been blessed with a small circle of friends but strongly reliable, trusting and reassuring individuals. They have been the voices of hope in my wilderness. They rose up to reassure me whilst in my lowest. They lifted me up not only with their presence but with their words. They created and spent time to cheer me up and assisted with childcare to allow me to have a break.

Friends have been the family that I do not have in the diaspora. They rally round me, pray for me, spent time with me and my children. They use their resources (time, presence, materials, finances, knowledge/information etc) to support me and the children. I have enjoyed authentic friendships most of the time. For this, I am eternally grateful,
I have never believed in a noisy crowd but in meaningful and positive interactions with a selected few. My friendship has been mostly intentional. I have sought friendship that is in alignment with my core values for the most part. No one does get friendship right 100% of the time, but mine has been meaningful to a good extent! I am very much aware of my areas of strength and weakness and those of my friendships and I have been able to navigate this road of friendship

carefully and purposefully. Our love and care for one another have been reciprocal. Relationships are gives and takes. To have good friends, you must be prepared to be a good one. It takes acceptance, respecting of boundaries, nurturing and sacrificing.

Being around people that are fostering of one's wellbeing is one of life's great pleasures; people that you can laugh with and be vulnerable with without losing your dignity. It's fun when I'm able to go out with friends. I didn't have a lot of opportunities to socialise with my friends when I was married, not even with ones that were also married, let alone the single ones! My friendships and interactions were stifled and controlled to a very high degree! I lost my individuality and independence. My man did not particularly believe that a married woman should be friends with single ladies. It's like once you're married, dump your single girls! It was not a view that I shared.

Upgrading my wardrobe became essential as I started to go out with friends again after thirteen years in a seeming lockdown. I had lost touch with how to be sensual and socialise in outings/parties from my late twenties all through my thirties. I started to use some make-up, jewellery, trousers etc. again after having been strictly forbidden to use these for thirteen years even though I was using all these when we met and before we married! It's a way of silencing, repackaging and forcefully subduing me whilst he continued to live his life with no restraint.

It's exciting and fun to dress up nicely for outings again. It's interesting for my kids to see me all done up. They weren't used to seeing Mum looking that beautiful in the old house. They take photos of me before I go out. They are always the stand by photographers. Few times, my daughter would put the photo up in her WhatsApp DP or shared it on Instagram. It's wonderful to be alive. It's fun! I have found some bits of flirting sometimes from men during outings interesting as it's shown that I'm still able to attract men even at my age and with my baggage and potential to date again! Getting the attention of men and dating are no longer as easy in your forties as they were in your twenties. I tried twice but realised I was not in the best position to foster the kind of meaningful relationship that I desire. I was not ready! I needed to work on myself more. I do believe that when it happens, it has the tendency to be a mature, meaningful and a mutually respectful relationship. It's a case of wine getting better with age, I want to believe! We shall see!

I have enjoyed the private/personal times I have spent with friends in meal outs, picnics, spa breaks, travels and indoors get-togethers than the ones spent in big parties and dos (Such as big weddings, birthdays, funerals etc.) even though I do recognise that these big parties and events are equally very important parts of life too. The indoor moments I have shared with some of my friends have been very fulfilling. The cooking or bring-a-dish or the take aways; washing and discussing TV programmes, dancing to music, chatting about our lives, our children and our men. Sharing our struggles at work and sometimes crying on each other's shoulders. Helping one another to relieve our individual/family struggles, including our stress and loneliness. It has been very reassuring and therapeutic.

Spending time with people that I trust has been a big part of my healing process. Mine have been very matured interactions. There has been no pressure on me by friends to go out and neither has there been pressure on them from me. Most of my friends are very busy individuals like myself. We do catch up regularly using different media and we do recognise when it's time to physically spend time together. Even though the current COVID season has significantly impacted on meetings, we have continued to remain in touch in as fun and creative ways as possible and have maintained our voices of hope.

Chapter 7
Looking Back – I Am Grateful

I have really come a long way, you know. The past nine years seem like an eternity. But I'm grateful for the progress that the children and I have made in our own different ways despite the everyday challenges. It's most times hard to believe where we currently are. The best achievement I have made in these years is in relation to my emotional wellbeing and stability, which has, in turn, helped me to raise my children and to hold down a job. I have learnt to primarily work on myself to become stronger and more resilient.

I'm a better person mentally and emotionally than I was when I was getting up from the rubbles. My confidence and self-esteem have improved to some extent. I am better able to make decisions without repeatedly questioning them. I have re-evaluated my values and worked on my boundaries. I have more clarity regarding the outcomes I desire in all aspects of my life especially my relationships, income and job.

I have modified my lifestyles in major ways to accommodate my change of circumstances. I attempt to keep my stress level and anxiety down from time to time. I have reached an improved level of calmness by paying attention to my general attitude to life, accepting what I cannot change, working on constructive feedback, being self-aware and able to look myself in the face and tackling negative and unproductive emotions, embracing my spirituality and factors fostering my positive wellbeing such as ensuring constructive social environments and friendships, keeping an eye on my physical health and activities, ensuring mental and cognitive stimulations, managing my income adequately and ensuring that I do not bite more that I can shew. Being in debt is one of the factors that can stress individuals significantly and rob them of their peace of mind.

I have learnt to focus my time and effort more on potentially positive outcomes, envisioning better realities for myself. I am better able to identify what are important for my children and I without apology about who I want to be or how I want to live. I have more control over my decisions and desired results. I have realised over these past years that my happiness in internal to me and only I can create my own happiness by aligning my expectations with my realities. And that even though material possessions or relationships can generate comfort, they cannot necessarily generate happiness. It's a state of being. I have to be happy in myself, just the way I am. Overall, I have a better attitude of peace and gratitude.

I am better able to put myself under checks whenever I begin to worry, become anxious, complain, compare or compete. I have learnt to concentrate on appreciating the little progress that I'm making from time to time whilst becoming a better version of myself. Ensuring that I'm not emotionally destabilised in any significant manner helps me to manage the two major tasks that I have got – raising my children and holding down a job.

The children have grown too. They've made major achievements in their education, in their personal and independent living skills and in the understanding of the world they live in. They are works in progress, just like I am. Improving in their self-esteem and identity, confidence, resilience and building and sustaining meaningful relationships are areas of ongoing growth that they will continue to learn on their own (guided by their own personal experiences) whilst I continue to encourage and support them as best possible. There is a need for me to manage my anxiety and to realise that they will become constructive and stable individuals who will contribute meaningfully to the society. I cannot protect them all their lives and stop them from making their own mistakes like I have done. Growth only comes from experiences, both positive and negative.

My job has evolved over the years as well, despite the struggles of having to balance work and life. I have put a lot of efforts into my various roles even though they have been very intensive, restrictive and structured for my personal circumstances. I have always pursued my job from a spiritual point of view... the Bible says, "Whatever your hand finds to do... do it with all your might..." (Eccl 9:10). My job has been a big part of my healing, not only in terms of providing focus and income, but largely to do with working in psychiatry environments. I use the strategies adopted at work in my own personal life to become better at fostering improved emotional and mental wellbeing.

Nonetheless, I have started to consider different ways of working in the recent years. As I am getting older, I want to work differently to increase my and my family's wellbeing. I have had difficulties with sustainable childminding since the autumn/fall of 2019. Complicating this even more is the COVID pandemic which has affected different sectors, including childcare.

The COVID also brought with it different creativities and innovations in the ways people work or want to work. My experiences, as I struggled to balance my work and life in the past months, have made me re-evaluate how I want to work in my fifties. I have realised that I do have control over how and where I want to work, despite being a carer for a child with disability. I do not want to be restricted to particular environments just because they make juggling my work and life somewhat manageable or they have the potentials to lead to promotions and more income, which are very good things anyway.

My perspectives have changed in the recent years, it's no longer about the big money or status, it's about peace and job satisfaction. I want to work differently in ways that align with my core values and will potentially foster these core values. Moving forward, I'd like to work with less structure and restrictions; with more flexibility, freedom and autonomy. My optimal goal will be to work from home, in full or in part. Even though I have always been a frontline worker, I'm strongly looking into working in a different setting within the health care sector. It sometimes feels daunting and impossible, but I keep on pushing forward in the directions of my goals despite various setbacks. I have concentrated on creating and bringing more values to my work. Values create more opportunities and make us irreplaceable in the marketplace.

Overall, there have been improvements in our lives as a family over the past years. We seem to have more clarity in relations to our goals despite everyday struggles and setbacks. We are concentrating on variables that are within our capabilities to control and leaving what we cannot control to God, as believers.

Chapter 8
One Day at a Time! –
The Journey Continues!

Now it's been nine years since the crash. A lot has happened over this period! I have been getting back on my feet, slowly but steadily. I still have a long way to go, I must say. I have continued to attempt to take one day at a time, as the saying goes. I have accepted my total package and I'm realistic of the expectations on myself and others. It's been my utmost need and desire to foster peace and harmony within my being. I am at my best when I'm less worried or stressed. I intend to align my everyday living with this core value of peace. I'm embracing different strategies to reduce my overall stress.

Spirituality and Mental Wellbeing

As a believer, I want to continue to improve my walk with God through Jesus Christ. Be more trusting of Him and in Him, with no doubt. I want to improve on that personal relationship! Just God and me! I want to get to the point where my peace and rest are rooted in Him regardless of the existing internal or external storms. I have continued to be aware of my everyday stressful or negative emotions and to challenge these in ways that have allowed me to continue to reframe my feelings and to re-write my story in ways that are less negative.

I also want to get more involved in Church and charity works, giving tangible things back to the society... my community. Volunteering, donations and fundraising are on my list of to do's even in my own little ways. They don't have to be massive! Every little act of kindness and humanity matter! I have always had the passion to volunteer with the elderlies; people with disabilities or befriend/advocate for lonely, vulnerable women!

Relationships and Social Interactions

I want to continue to review my relationships and circles of influence whether socially or professionally. I don't want to stay in a relationship or environment that is no longer fostering or has become toxic to my physical or mental wellbeing regardless of other benefits it may contain. I want to spend time in activities including a job with positive and well-meaning people... the ones that align with my spirit and heart... the ones that excite, expand and motivate me... not ones that drag me down or weigh down my energy and make me to become unsure of myself... certainly not ones that generate anxiety and dread in me. For example, I wouldn't want to stay in a job where I'm mostly unhappy because it affords me security, money, status or promotion!

I want to pursue my own happiness and quality of life even if the money is not that great. I don't want to continue to remain in a relationship whether intimate or platonic because I'm afraid of being alone. It's good to sometimes be alone or do things alone. To develop depth within oneself. To develop one's own sense of meaning, autonomy and independence.

Managing Finances

It's important to improve my finances. It'd be wonderful to make money, have savings and investments, but it's much more important to me to not be in debts. To be able to manage the resources available to me. To live within my means. To not make unnecessary spendings driven by needs to go with the media, retail sectors, fashion and trends or needs to be validated by the expectations of social circles or friends. Being in debt has been widely described as having the capacity to cause a lot of stress and worry: impacting negatively on mental health, causing feelings of shame and embarrassment and sometimes making it problematic to meet basic everyday needs. I have been in an environment where receiving default letters was an everyday occurrence and I have looked after individuals with debts issues. I know first-hand how stressful these issues can be! I try to avoid getting trapped in this web! I make sure I pay all my bills, including a credit-card first. Fulfilling these obligations first reduces my stress and allows me to focus on managing what I am left with.

Not Waiting for Others to Rescue Me

Making my own decisions, validating myself and taking responsibilities for my own actions are what I intend to continue to focus on moving forward. There is no one to rescue me... I need to continue to strive on my own relying on God's strength. Even if there is a rescuer somewhere, it can only be a bonus! It's not about sitting and waiting for others to set me free or make ways for me; it's unrealistic and irresponsible to put one's destiny in the hands of other people. I have heard different ladies waiting and hoping for men that'd help sort out their, and their children's, lives! Don't get me wrong, no one is an island. People need help in whatever way, form or shape from time to time. But ultimately, you've got to map out your own routes and take chances! Take positive risks! I want to continue to make decisions that have high probability of fostering peace and tranquillity within me, regardless of whether or not they are validated by others.

Managing Physical Health

It's very important that I continue to pay attention to my physical health, especially as I'm growing older. It's not always easy to be on top of all these PH issues but I do try and I'm very clued up as to what I need to do. I'm aware of when I'm having setbacks. I pay attention to my diets and ensure that they are as healthy as possible. Sometimes people think you've got to spend a lot of money to buy fad foods to be healthy or to buy from the highest part of the supermarket shelves. But it's not necessarily the case! There are a lot of our everyday products that are healthy and tasty. All you need to do is to be creative and to reduce the sinful bits such sugar, salt, fats/oil etc. I have found paying attention to portions, frequency and timing very helpful in managing my weight. I have to confess that I've not been eating fruits as much as I should, given that they are always available for the children. But I eat a lot of vegetables/salad with my meals and drink a lot of water or herbal teas. Wine is OK for me from time to time, but I tend not to indulge in a lot of alcohol when alone. I mostly drink alcohol when I'm with friends. I enjoy it better in social situations and reasonably too.

Oh, how can I forget about vitamins. Glorious vitamins! I take some vitamins, mostly Vit-B, C and D, Iron, and some vitamins for guts in forms of yogurts or so. I don't know if they necessarily work in any significant way but they sure don't cause any harm either. I have convinced myself that they are benefiting me, even in minor ways, especially the Vitamin-D, which, I have read, that it's particularly beneficial for Black people.

I make sure that I exercise regularly. I have not been to the gym in the last few years but mostly commuting has helped me to keep fit to some extent. Walking has been very good to both my physical and mental health. It helps to clear my head as it helps to clear my fat! During core COVID-19 months, more and more inspirational videos of fitness and exercises sprung up on the Internet/YouTube. They were welcome and mostly free too! Even though I'm on prescription medications for high blood pressure, which I do comply with, I have found that my blood pressure is mostly manageable when I'm peaceful and calm inside… when stress and conflicts are reduced.

I ensure that I check myself up regularly and attend all my hospital/doctors' appointments. If I'm uncomfortable about any health issue, whether for myself or my kids, I don't stop until I get to the bottom of it. I'm very much aware though that this is easier in one part of the world than others.

I try to look after my teeth, hair and skin regularly as well. I don't use strong products but everyday mild items that my body can tolerate, including water based skin products. I also use some oil products such as olive or coconut. My use of makeup is very minimal but I do try, especially if I have a function to attend. I have always fantasised about having well-manicured finger nails like some ladies. But as much as I envy these, they do not fit into my everyday routine, both at home or at work. I cut my nails regularly and try to file them but they could do with more TLC. My eyes are not as sharp as they used to be. They are weakened by many years of weariness and tears. I go for check-ups every two years to review and also to review my prescription glasses.

Perimenopause is what I'm currently having to deal with, in fact, I have been dealing with it since 2015 when I first experienced my first hot flush! It's an unusual feeling and I had to secretly call on a female colleague, who explained what it was and said, "Welcome to the club." I have explored a number of information and have found that it affects individuals differently. There are about thirty-four different symptoms. In my case, I have been dealing with the hot flushes, heavy and irregular periods and night sweats more than the other issues such as anxiety, mood swings, etc. I am just taking them as they come. It can also feel emotional knowing that one's woman cycle is gradually coming to an end but it's my hope and desire to live each season of my life optimally. This is my current season... welcome!

Managing My Older Years

Growing older comes with a number of different changes but I intend to continue to look up as I'm getting along. I want to hold on to a sense of being useful with opportunities to continue to be stimulated and to have joy in my life. I want to connect more broadly and dare to step out of my comfort zones, which has always been a struggle. I do not want to yield to the stamp that society puts on people in their fifties or sixties. I plan to continue to maximise my potentials and to live my life to the fullest, whatever that means to me! I don't want to throw myself away and become irrelevant. I want to continue to do things on my own or with other happy, trusting and meaningful friendships when the chances present themselves.

Each day, I think about different things I could be doing. Ideas pop up in my mind or sometimes, I think about old dreams that have never been achieved but could still be, even if in slightly different ways, given the current seasons and trends. I want to learn to reinvent myself as I'm getting older. I want to rekindle my passions. Looking into my untapped resources; my unused skills; find something that I don't know how to do; something I want to improve at to better myself… something to keep the wheels rolling! Improving my skills in the areas of my dreams and passions. I have been seriously looking into how I can tap into technology in this 21st century. It seems to be the main thing now, especially because of COVID19.

There's a saying that goes, "Old ways may not open new doors." I have started to embrace some technological inventions that can make life a bit easier… in my own little ways. Putting my credit card on my mobile/cell phone for easy access. Sometimes I forget my bank card at home but I never forget my mobile phone. Online banking saves me time. I have only been to bank in a very few times in many years. Online shopping helps me to manage my time. My CV is on my mobile, at hand at all times and also on an online CV library. Hey Google – Echo dot – to ask for information when I'm being too lazy to go on the internet. It's probably the coolest invention for me in the recent months. A friend actually bought it for me as a birthday present. My Bluetooth speakers – small but mighty. I take it with me when I go to the parks with the kids. We listen to music and dance together. My mobile – on the go – phone charger. That one too, very useful!

There is still a lot to learn or overcome as far as maximising the use of technology is concerned. I have never been drawn to a massive use of social media such as Facebook, Twitter, IG, etc. And I don't know whether or not I'd cross those bridges at some points. Who knows? I do look at my children's pages from time to time, when they want to show me their work. But I have personally found accesses to YouTube's material very beneficial to my overall healing and growth. And I have kept a small number of close social contacts on my WhatsApp. It's a space that I have held very private. I have been trying to learn how to play Wii or X-Box or PSG with my children, but I never quite got there yet. I felt like it's very important to be able to also connect with them in this way as millennial kids. Technology is the new age and it's useful to embrace it to a useful and meaningful extent. My fiftieth birthday was technologically informed in spring, 2020. It was one borne out of the restrictions of lockdown in the core months of COVID-19 pandemic. Even though I was at home with my children, it was fun and creative to be able to connect remotely with friends and family here and abroad. It was probably the most fun birthday I have had in a long time, despite the lockdown!

I have been stepping out of my comfort zone in other areas as well. Within reason, in alignment with my true self. I started to wear synthetic hair with colours. Hurray! Can you believe that? I have always been a traditional person who'd feel comfortable in only black wigs, as my natural hair colour is black. Stark black! But these days, I have been wearing some synthetics with bits of colour blends. Bits of brown, grey/silver, gold, purple or burgundy sometimes! Who would have ever thought! Oh yes, I shouldn't forget that I had one of my upper ear lobes pierced as well. Now I don a tiny bling-bling stud from time to time. Nice, isn't it? It's a wonderful feeling to be able to make my choices! To live my authentic life with no duress. To express myself the way I deem fit.

I have kept on going by God's grace. Some days are better than the others. Finding the motivation and drive are big parts of my moving on. To be honest, It's most times difficult. But I have found that it'd continue to be if I don't fan the flames of my passion. I have found that whatever I need to do must resonate with my deepest values even if it does not generate more income or status. They must foster my authentic self. Those interests that are purposeful… connections to something that are larger than me. I have a list of different ideas. I add to these from time to time. Writing is something that I have always done, even as a child and to write books is one of my dreams. But I've got to start somewhere! After having put this off for many years, using one excuse or the other, I eventually started to put pen to paper (or rather fingers to key pads) in the September of 2020. That birthed this memoir!

Learning from the Experiences of My Mother

The illness and the eventual death of my mother in 2020 provided me huge perspectives about life. Learning to live everyday with gratitude and hope. Even though no child wants to lose their parent(s), it was the illness of my mum that I found more painful. The illness that robbed her of living... of enjoying little things of life, especially in retirement and in her old age.

I learnt a lot from her experiences that are informing how I intend to live my life moving forward. To live each day as though it were the last... to appreciate little things of life... to enjoy the presence of those who cheer you on... to not have the expectation that certain people will be around and will hold you all through your journey... to be OK with knowing that those you thought would watch your back may not be available for whatever reasons.

Maximising the COVID Season

The COVID season crept in, unannounced, and impacted the lives of millions of people all over the world, including mine and my family. The effects differ from people to people. Some sadly lost their friends and families; some lost their means of livelihood; some lost their properties; some had to learn to work in different ways; some have had to work at the frontline, despite the serious risks, whilst majority of people became isolated and separated from their loved ones. The fear, anxiety and loneliness borne out of being unable to share lives with others are probably the greatest impacts of the pandemic. The fear of being alone, with no support from friends and family should you need them… the fear of keeping yourself and immediate family safe from infection… the stress of having to monitor your children's education provision, the stress of dealing with school closures and isolations, COVID testing for you and family and navigating this with individuals with autism and LD, uncertainty that pervades the whole atmosphere and the fear of the unknown future! What will be our new normal, no one knows. But certainly, the world as we knew it has changed! The pandemic changed the world's perspectives on personal, communal and global levels.

Despite the challenges of year 2020, I attempted to create some positivity in my mind from time to time. I have tried to manage my fears and anxieties. It's very difficult to do these but I had to… for the benefits of my children and also because of my day job which requires me to give hope to the hopeless most times. I started to tell myself that something positive can come out of this darkness. That even in this difficult season, some people have realised their dreams of returning to education, of becoming parents for the first time, of marrying, starting a new business, improving their income, improving their health, getting promotion at work, improving in their values and character, buying a new house… and writing their first book! I pushed myself to start writing this book, which I have written in my head many times! There's a need for me to tell my stories!

Using My Experiences to Benefit Others

There must be something for others to benefit or learn from all of my own experiences, regardless of how little! I started to volunteer two hours per week in a care/group home for the elderlies. I listened to their experiences and they listened to mine. It's very enriching! This has been disrupted by the current COVID policies. Hopefully, I'll return. I have added two more to my charity fundraising/donation works in the recent years. I'm getting better and better each day.

Writing this book is one of the many ways that others may also benefit from my experiences. And that's why you have read this memoir to the end... to the last page. I hope something positive, elevating or inspiring has stayed with you! I hope you can make a connection and realise that you are not alone. It has helped me to clear my head and made me feel lighter. It's hard sometimes when you have all these materials embedded internally. It's like de-cluttering... I feel at ease! Talking about de-cluttering, I think I need to sort out my immediate environment as well!

Anyhow, life continues, and it's for living. Finding gratitude in daily experiences can be very helpful. Keep living, keep the resilience and hope going!

CPSIA information can be obtained
at www.ICGtesting.com
Printed in the USA
BVHW031424270622
640731BV00012B/267